TRIBULATION
TO TRIUMPH
A Mandate for Today's Church

TRIBULATION TO TRIUMPH
A Mandate for Today's Church

by
Rod Parsley

Harrison House
Tulsa, Oklahoma

TRIBULATION TO TRIUMPH:
A Mandate for Today's Church
ISBN 0-89274-881-8
Copyright © 1991 by Rod Parsley
World Harvest Church
P. O. Box 32932
Columbus, Ohio 43232

Published by Harrison House, Inc.
P. O. Box 35035
Tulsa, Oklahoma 74153

DEDICATION

This book is affectionately dedicated to my daughter, Ashton Blaire, who was born just as the first tremors of the "shaking" began. It is my prayer that she and her generation come to the certainty of Christ Jesus and join her mother, Joni, and I in the preparation of His Church.

CONTENTS

FOREWORD

For Rod Parsley to invite me to write the foreword to this book is an honor. His ministry is reaching out over the nation through television and personal appearances of preaching in conventions and churches. His church in Columbus, Ohio, has experienced remarkable growth in the last few years. He is part of that prophetic word in Acts Chapter 2, Verse 17: **And it shall come to pass in the last days, saith God, I will pour out of my Spirit upon all flesh: and your sons and your daughters shall prophesy, and your young men shall see visions, and your old men shall dream dreams.**

The message of this book is very exciting and can be said many ways. For example, you have to plow the ground before you can have a beautiful harvest. The ground may look very ugly all plowed up, but it is necessary for a new harvest. Mechanics will tell you that sometimes you have to take a car apart only to put it together again for it to function properly. There are times when one has to go through very trying moments in order to triumph.

In his introduction, Pastor Parsley puts his finger on the key to true victory in the Church. He has dealt with holiness in our personal lives. Israel never backslid until they had fullness of bread and plenty of prosperity. Our Church today has ample material blessings and has great need of spiritual cleansing from the pulpit and the pew.

As one of our younger men reaching out to God and to the world, it is notable that he is deeply concerned regarding spiritual integrity, especially in our Church relationship. The Lord has told me that you preach what you get. If we do not preach holiness and if we do not preach hell for those who miss Heaven, we will not have the proper relationships with our God. There is a world of revival in many nations facing us, and there may be persecution for all of us. For us to be strong in the Lord and the power of His might, we must believe that God wants only a holy Church.

May the message of this book inspire you, bless you and give you a conscience void of offense toward God. May God bless Rod Parsley as he ventures into the future, and God bless you who read and study this book.

Lester Sumrall
South Bend, Indiana

INTRODUCTION

Change is imperative for the church of our generation. Although we have erected sanctuaries, raised millions of dollars and elevated ministries to international heights, we have also managed, in the process, to lower our standards. The general church has become so preoccupied with its efforts to get the message out, that we have all but forgotten what The Message is.

Of late, we have used our fingers to point to our own efforts, instead of the cross. We have busied our hands patting each other on the back, instead of laying our hands on those who need prayer.

It is imperative for us to stop, to take a step back, and check our foundation, because there is a shaking coming. The Church is about to be purged of her impurities. The Lord God will return for a bride who is without spot or blemish. And if we are not ready, we will be shaken off the cornerstone with the rest of the chaff.

When the shaking is over and the dust clears, I don't intend to be found lying underneath the rubble of impurity left behind. . . Do you?

To survive the trials just ahead, the Church has to be strong. Yet to triumph over the coming tribulations we also have to be smart. It is time for the Church of Jesus Christ to wake up . . . and prepare!

Pastor Rod Parsley
Columbus, Ohio

TRIBULATION
TO TRIUMPH
A Mandate for Today's Church

TRIBULATION
TO TRIUMPH

PART
One

"To survive we've got to be strong..."

The Church:
A Crumbling Structure?

"I have something to say to you
— and the Church."

CHAPTER
I

In the fall of 1989 I took my wife on a short vacation to Florida. It was to be a quiet time before the Lord, an occasion for Him to clarify to my spirit the things I had been sensing. For a long while, it seemed, the words of Luke 21 had echoed in my head, . . . **the days will come, in the which there shall not be left one stone upon another** . . . It was imperative for me to get away, to rest, and allow God the opportunity to communicate.

However, when the Lord finally did speak a few days later, the time He chose and the method He used were almost as surprising as the message itself.

That particular evening, I had switched on the TV in anticipation of watching the third game of the World Series being played in San Francisco. Yet as the blue-white light of the TV set illuminated my room, my eyes did not focus on a baseball stadium filled with cheering fans. To my astonishment I saw ambulances, fire trucks and people running in panic.

The game had been called off by a cataclysmic event — an earthquake registering 6.9 on the Richter scale. As my ears began to tune in to what my eyes were seeing, I became aware of a reporter's voice expressing the fear that thousands of people in the Bay area had been lost or seriously injured. The estimated property damage was in the billions.

I saw large stretches of freeways, tons of steel and concrete, literally flapping in the breeze. Steel suspension bridges had been snapped in two, and automobiles were flattened into nothing.

The video replays of security cameras in local stores showed people quietly going about their business. One lady was reaching for a can of green peas, another was squeezing a head of lettuce, when suddenly they froze as the ground underneath their feet began to move. Items on surrounding shelves and counters began to fall. Instantly, store patrons began to scream and run in every direction, as chunks of walls and ceilings fell around them.

As I sat transfixed, witnessing this scene of destruction, the chaotic sounds from the TV faded and I began to hear the Holy Spirit whisper, "I have brought you here specifically at this time because I have something to say to you — and the Church. . . ."

Listening to the Spirit, I felt Him guide me once again to the unique story found at the beginning of Luke 21. As Jesus and His disciples approached the Jerusalem temple, they paused. In that brief interval the attention of a few of the men was drawn to the immense size and beauty of the nearby edifice. Shading their eyes from the glare of the bright Palestinian sun, the men gazed up at the temple and admired its stately height and breadth.

Like a group of awe-stricken tourists, the disciples began pointing out to each other particularly interesting features. They praised the natural beauty and craftsmanship of the temple which had taken forty-six years to complete. (John 2:20.)

Finally, after hearing enough of their mortal observations of the physical, Jesus spoke up. In one simple sentence, He pointed out to His followers an important feature they could not see...the realm of the Spirit.

> As for these things which ye behold, the days will come, in the which there shall not be left one stone upon another, that shall not be thrown down.
>
> Luke 21:6

Close to forty years after these words were spoken, Christ's prophecy was violently fulfilled, when in A.D. 70 the Roman army destroyed Jerusalem, demolishing the temple and scattering the Jews throughout the world.

What Jesus was saying to His followers then is the same thing I believe the Holy Spirit is saying to us in the Church today; "Your churches may have been built to the glory of God, but remember — they are constructed by human hands, out of mortar and stone. When the tremors of tribulation come, not one of your temporal structures will remain intact."

The message of Christ's words are clear; his instructions to the disciples (as well as to today's materialistic church) were to get their eyes off of the physical world and focus on the things of the Spirit. One day, the great palaces and monuments of this natural world will all crumble and fall, but the things of the Spirit will last forever.

Although beautiful edifices are being constructed in the name of Jesus today, many in recent years have been erected as a monument to man's achievement. I believe, for this reason, the Church has already undergone the preliminary jolt of two public scandals.

Our attentions have been focused more on our accomplishments in the physical world than on our responsibilities to the things of God. Like the disciples, many Christians have paused along the way to admire the achievements of the Church. "Just look at all we've done!"

However, when we stop to applaud such material things, we waste precious moments. Physical things are temporal. They have a time limit. And the clock is running out on the earthly endeavors of the Church.

I fear that if we don't heed Christ's correction now and open up our spiritual eyes, the rumble that is coming in the nineties will catch us as off guard and unprepared as the victims of San Francisco's quake.

Check Your Foundation

If we are not ready when the needle of the spiritual Richter scale flies off the dial, the Church will be shaken right down to its foundation. The tremors we have felt up to now are nothing compared to what is coming.

When the Lord returns, He's coming back for a Church that is completely devoid of all spot and blemish. Every foundation will be shaken. Is our foundation constructed of things temporal or eternal? Is our cornerstone built by man or God?

If we have constructed our life on the foundation of a man's personality, we will be shaken off it. If our marriages are built only on the temporal base of outward beauty, that foundation will crack. If our relationships are based solely on the security of a weekly, physical paycheck, that support will splinter.

It is time the people of the Church realize that only the spiritual structures of faith, hope and love will endure. (1 Cor. 13:13.) It is time Christians get their eyes off the natural and turn them back to Jesus. It is imperative that we get firmly planted in the bedrock of God's timeless Holy Word, so that we might become the spotless Church that Christ is returning to reclaim.

Purification by Tribulation

As I sat in front of the television that evening, listening to the Holy Spirit and watching the terrible aftermath of a natural disaster, I recalled the words God said to the prophet Jeremiah:

> . . .I have this day set thee over the nations AND
> over the kingdoms, to root out, and to pull down, and
> to destroy, and to throw down, to build, and to plant.
> Jeremiah 1:10

19

Thinking about this passage, I realized that *tribulation produces strength*. It "roots out" the imperfections. It destroys the fragile.

As I watched the news report of sad losses and heroic rescues during the San Francisco quake, it became obvious to me that *adversity makes the strong stronger — and the weak weaker*.

I came to the conclusion that the destruction and carnage I was witnessing on live TV was an example of the shaking the Christian world was about to experience.

Just as God perfected Jeremiah's generation by "pulling down" — then building, He is likewise cranking up the purifying process for us today. Before the foundation of *this* generation of Christians can be confirmed as solid, it will be shaken to remove all of the impurities. The strong will become stronger — but the weak *will not survive*.

The Church of today must be prepared for the tribulations that lie ahead. If we concentrate on admiring the temporal, spending our time reading a can of green peas and squeezing a few heads of lettuce, we are not only wasting the precious time God has given us, but we run the risk of being caught off guard when the shaking starts.

When Satan attacks, I don't want to freeze in my tracks. I don't want to scream and run aimlessly for cover. I want to be the kind of Christian who senses the danger and instinctively knows by the Spirit what measures must be taken to combat the onslaught.

When the shaking is over and the dust of the battle clears, I want to be the one left standing, don't you? Every born-again, sanctified, Holy Ghost-filled, Bible-believing Christian has the ability to withstand all the devil can dish out, and more. The Church of Jesus Christ has been given all the power necessary to turn tribulation into triumph.

How can we acquire this power? By getting our eyes off the temporal and turning our attention to things eternal. We must learn how to walk in the Spirit.

Walk in the Spirit

> But there is a spirit in man: and the inspiration
> of the Almighty giveth them understanding.
>
> Job 32:8

God gave man two endowments that no other earthly creation possesses: *a spirit* — the only part of us that is truly eternal, and *the power of free will.* In doing so, the Creator placed in us, His creation, the ability to *choose freely* whether to be ruled by our temporal body, which will one day die and decay, or to be directed by our *eternal* spirit, which can lead us to life everlasting.

I don't know why anyone, given such choices, would want to spend his entire life dominated by a physical force that is destined to decay. It's a hard thing to comprehend, but millions make that fateful decision every day.

So how does one go about making the choice for the Spirit? Jesus told Nicodemus, . . . except a man be born again, he cannot see the kingdom of God (John 3:3). He was not talking about going back into your mother's womb and starting over again — that's looking at things

21

from the *physical* perspective. As usual, the Son of God was referring to the *spiritual* alternative.

That which is born of the flesh, Jesus explained, **is flesh** . . . God formed man from the dust of the earth, therefore, from our mother's womb, *our flesh is a part of this world.*

. . . **and that which is born of the Spirit is spirit.** (John 3:6). To be born of the Spirit requires the power of a free will to believe. If your choice is to walk in the Spirit, *faith* is a basic necessity. But what are we to believe?

. . . **God so loved the world, that he gave his only begotten Son, that whosoever believeth in him should not perish, but have everlasting life** (John 3:16).

This is the cornerstone, the solid foundation on which every Christian life should be based. However, in the Church today there are those who *claim* to believe in the saving power of Christ, and confess that they lean on the Holy Spirit for direction, yet still keep one eye sharply focused on the physical.

We *are* a *spirit* and we *live* in a *body,* but these shaky Christians live as if they *are* a body and *have* a spirit. They give more attention to what their *body is doing to them* than what *their spirit can do to their body.* They say they are walking in the Spirit, but in reality they are wandering in a fog.

Why do great, highly anointed preachers get sick, die, or fall into a sin that destroys their ministry? It is because they preach in the Spirit *but do not live in the Spirit.*

How can Christians be filled with the Holy Ghost, sit under the teaching of the Word, sing and praise God and still live in poverty, sickness and tragedy? Simple: such people worship in the Spirit, but *live* in the flesh. They are shaky and undisciplined.

A born-again child of God does *not* have to sin. I've heard some people say with a smile, "The devil made me do it." *My Christian friend, the devil cannot make you do anything without your cooperation. He doesn't have the authority!*

Those who continually allow their attention to be drawn away from the Spirit and back into the physical world are undisciplined and weak. Without God's help, the weak become weaker when tribulations come!

A church made up of such impurity will never survive the shaking that's coming. It's time we opened our eyes, checked our foundation and renewed our resolve.

Just as the disciples did not readily see what Christ saw in the spirit, shaky Christians are so blinded by their physical problems that they cannot see the spiritual arsenal God has provided them.

Why is the Church still running from the victory? Our side has already won! Have we collectively forgotten that the Son of God died and rose again to retrieve our birthright of dominion? Has it slipped our minds that when we accepted Christ we became a part of the family of God?

Then let me remind you that if we, as Christians, are obedient, live *daily* according to the Word of God and look to Him, as our Lord and provider, we won't have to wander in search of His blessings — they will *overtake* us!

Take a moment to examine this "brief" list in Deuteronomy 28 of blessing God has promised the obedient:

> And it shall come to pass, *if thou shalt hearken diligently unto the voice of the Lord thy God, to observe and to do all his commandments———the Lord thy God will* set thee on high above all nations of the earth: and all these blessings shall come on thee, and overtake thee... Blessed shalt thou be in the city, and blessed shalt thou be in the field. Blessed shall be the fruit of thy body, and the fruit of thy ground, and the fruit of thy cattle... Blessed shall be thy basket and thy store. Blessed shalt thou be when thou comest in, and blessed shalt thou be when thou goest out.
>
> *The Lord shall cause thine enemies that rise up against thee to be smitten before thy face: they shall come out against thee one way, and flee before thee seven ways.* The Lord shall command the blessing upon thee in thy storehouses, and in all that thou settest thine hand unto... and all people of the earth shall see that thou art called by the name of the Lord; and they shall be afraid of thee... *the Lord shall open unto thee his good treasure*———thou shalt lend unto many nations, and thou shalt not borrow. *And the Lord shall make thee the head, and not the tail; and thou shalt be above only, and thou shalt not be beneath;* if that thou hearken unto the commandments of the Lord thy God..
>
> Deuteronomy 28:1-8,10,12,13

Our God is a mighty God! He is Jehovah-Jireh, our provider — the God Who is more than enough. There is no reason why the Church should look to any other source for sustenance, security or salvation. We are the Church, the body of Jesus Christ — and it's time we started acting like it — before it's too late!

Before Another Stone Is Shaken

That night, as I watched the ambulances scream away with the broken bodies of those salvaged from San Francisco's quake, I sensed that the needle of the spiritual Richter scale would soon begin to flutter. The Church must get ready.

We all must check our foundation and resolve anew to get our eyes off of Satan's lies — and back onto the prize!

When the tremors of the coming tribulation have passed and the damage to the Body of Christ is assessed, I don't want to be found pinned under the rubble of the discarded impurities. I want to be *strong* going in and *even stronger* coming out. The only way to accomplish that is to stay ready, use God's time wisely and walk daily in the Spirit.

On that memorable evening not so long ago, the Holy Spirit whispered, ". . . I have something to say to you — and the Church." Just as with the disciples, in one simple sentence God began to point our attention to that which we cannot see. Before another stone is shaken out of place, shouldn't we listen and learn?

When the dust of the quake is over, will we have heeded God's instruction and triumphed over tribulation? Or will there be a sign nailed to the unhinged door of the Church:

**STRUCTURE UNSOUND: FOUNDATION CRACKED
THIS BUILDING IS...CONDEMNED.**

The answer is up to you.

The Trials of Tribulation

"They courageously looked death in the face
and proclaimed the certainty of eternal life."

CHAPTER
II

Nebuchadnezzar said to them, Is it true, O Shadrach, Meshach, and Abednego, that you do not serve my gods, or worship the golden image which I have set up?

Now if you are ready when you hear the sound of the horn, pipe, lyre, trigon, harp, dulcimer, or bagpipe, and every kind of music to fall down and worship the image which I have made, very good. But if you do not worship, you shall be cast at once into the midst of a burning fiery furnace, and who is that god who can deliver you out of my hands?

Shadrach, Meshach and Abednego answered the king, O Nebuchadnezzar, it is not necessary for us to answer you on this point.

If our God Whom we serve is able to deliver us from the burning fiery furnace, He will deliver us out of your hand, O king.

But if not, let it be known to you, O king, that we will not serve your gods, or worship the golden image which you have set up.

Then Nebuchadnezzar was full of fury and his facial expression was changed to [antagonism] against Shadrach, Meshach, and Abednego. Therefore he commanded that the furnace should be heated seven times hotter than it was usually heated.

And he commanded the strongest men in his army to bind Shadrach, Meshach and Abednego and to cast them into the burning fiery furnace.

Then these three men were bound in their cloaks, their tunics or undergarments, their turbans, and their other clothing, and they were cast into the midst of the burning fiery furnace.

Daniel 3:14-21 AMP

I don't know what it was about those Old Testament days, but the men and women who served God back then seemed to have a "certain something." Although they often faced the roaring fires of tribulation, they kept their shields of faith held high. And even on those particularly trying occasions when the flames were so overpowering that even their shields became too hot to handle, they held on anyway.

Their stubborn commitment to the precepts of God provided this special few with the necessary courage to speak before the great and small. If they had to step on the toes of the powerful, they did it. If they had to stretch out their necks over the chopping block, they were willing. Like Shadrach, Meshach and Abednego, these "certain-something" saints stood their ground and yielded to *nothing* — except God's will.

From the Old Testament prophets to the New Testament Church, God has always had a stubborn, select few who bravely valued spiritual truth more than their own physical safety.

> And the Spirit of God came upon Zechariah the son of Jehoiada the priest, which stood above the people, and said unto them, Thus saith God, Why transgress ye the commandments of the Lord, that ye cannot prosper? because ye have forsaken the Lord, he hath also forsaken you.
>
> And they conspired against him, and stoned him with stones at the commandment of the king, in the court of the house of the Lord.
>
> 2 Chronicles 24:20,21

The attack on Zechariah was not an isolated incident. Throughout the Old Testament whenever the truth was obediently declared, there was always immediate opposition.

It takes a special breed of people not only to speak the gospel willingly, but also to face voluntarily the fires of tribulation that follow. Those courageous prophets of old were indeed a persevering bunch.

> And what shall I say further? For time would fail me to tell of Gideon, Barak, Samson, Jephthah, of David and Samuel and the prophets.

Who by [the help of] faith subdued kingdoms, administered justice, obtained promised blessings, closed the mouths of lions,

Extinguished the power of raging fire, escaped the devourings of the sword, out of frailty and weakness won strength and became stalwart, even mighty and resistless in battle, routing alien hosts.

[Some] women received again their dead by a resurrection. Others were tortured to death with clubs, refusing to accept release [offered on the terms of denying their faith], that they might be resurrected to a better life.

Others had to suffer the trial of mocking and scourging, and even chains and imprisonment.

They were stoned to death; they were lured with tempting offers [to renounce their faith]; they were sawn asunder; they were slaughtered by the sword; [while they were alive] they had to go about wrapped in the skins of sheep and goats, utterly destitute, oppressed, cruelly treated.

[Men] of whom the world was not worthy, roaming over the desolate places and the mountains, and [living] in caves and caverns and holes of the earth (AMP)...having obtained a good report through faith...(KJV)

Hebrews 11:32-39 AMP, KJV

The early Church did not have it any easier — in fact, by most accounts, the tribulations of those first devout Christians were exceptionally violent, inhuman and frequent.

Take for instance the events surrounding Christianity's first martyr:

Dragged before a powerful group of rabbis and members of the council, Stephen, a young church leader, was forced to defend himself against false accusations. Facing his angry accusers, this brilliant "man of faith" eloquently proclaimed his convictions. And despite the growing anger of his audience, he stood his ground and boldly spoke the truth.

> You stubborn and stiff-necked people, still heathenish and uncircumcised in heart and ears, you are always actively resisting the Holy Spirit. As your forefathers were, so you are and so you do!

> Which of the prophets did your forefathers not persecute? And they slew those who proclaimed beforehand the coming of the Righteous One, Whom you now have betrayed and murdered,

> You who received the Law as it was ordained and set in order and delivered by angels, and yet you did not obey it!

> Now upon hearing these things, they [the Jews] were cut to the heart and infuriated, and they ground their teeth against Stephen.

> But he, full of the Holy Spirit and controlled by Him, gazed into heaven and saw the glory — the splendor and majesty — of God, and Jesus standing at God's right hand;

> And he said, Look! I see the heavens opened, and the Son of man standing at God's right hand!

But they raised a great shout and put their hands over their ears and rushed together upon him.

Then they dragged him out of the city and began to stone him, and witnesses placed their garments at the feet of a young man named Saul.

Acts 7:51-58 AMP

It is ironic — Christianity's first martyr was dispatched by the "church" itself. Although the rocks the Council threw that day were not the temple stones to which Christ referred in Luke 21, they were nonetheless blocks seized from one corner of the building's foundation to bring about the demolition of another corner. On hand to witness the deed was an extremely pleased Saul, the official "church" representative, dedicated to that destructive purpose.

Like the stone throwers of the Jerusalem synagogue, there are churches today that have allowed themselves to become so earthbound by the physical traditions of men that their spiritual insight is gone. The anointing has left them. Their foundation has split in two.

When these legalistic churches see a body of believers that are led by the Holy Spirit — and not ashamed to say so — they complain, point accusing fingers and throw stones of discord. Such religious organizations have become so earthly minded that they are of no heavenly good. The analogy is clear: *a house divided against itself cannot stand.*

To avoid the fate that awaits these mausoleums of tradition, we must consider Stephen's reaction to the bone-crushing blows of the stones, and act accordingly.

And he kneeled down, and cried with a loud
voice, Lord lay not this sin to their charge. And when
he had said this, he fell asleep.

Acts 7:60

Stephen had that "certain something." His foundation
was sure. Even as his blood and breath were being pounded
out of his broken body, he did not focus on temporal
things, but turned his eyes to the sky, and his attention
to things eternal.

...Behold, I see the heavens opened, and the
Son of man standing on the right hand of God.

Acts 7:56

The martyrdom of Stephen was just the beginning.
Thousands followed. However, this young man would
never have had the courage to proclaim his faith, neither
would the Church have had the tenacity to endure the
satanic punishments that were just ahead, if they did not
possess that collective "certain something."

That rare quality was a "certainty" of faith — the
assurance of absolute fact. The early Christian Church
knew, without a doubt, that their cause was just — and
true! Many of the faithful faced the slings and arrows of
outrageous tribulation with a first hand picture of Christ's
earthly ministry etched across their mind's eye. They knew
with a certainty in Whom they believed.

If their faith had been based on a myth or an
exaggerated tale, Christianity would have fizzled after the
first wave of bloodletting. Who in his right mind would

attempt to convince an angry, stone-toting mob of a baseless, unprovable fable?

But that was not the case. In the face of horrifying punishment, the faithful flourished. They were driven by an overwhelming desire to tell what they saw, what they heard and what they experienced.

Yet this knowledge and desire did not come easily. Whenever the light of truth begins to shine, the opposition always throws up a blanket of darkness to snuff it out. Such was the case with the early Church. Just as the certainty of Christ's light began to illuminate the Judean hills, a sudden darkness appeared, and the bright hope of all who believed faded to black.

Certainty in the Dark

To the disciples it seemed as if everything was over. Feeling helpless and despondent, they stood off at a distance and watched as the Light of their world faded before their eyes.

Nailed to a cross were all their hopes and dreams. Their reason for living hung before them bleeding and dying. And as if things were not dark enough, the sky above them was turning black in the middle of the day.

> And it was about the sixth hour, and there was a darkness over all the earth until the ninth hour.
>
> And the sun was darkened, and the veil of the temple was rent in the midst.
>
> Luke 23:44,45

Looking at the blood-stained body of Jesus, the disciples shook their heads in dismay. They had seen this Man give sight to the blind. They had watched Him open deaf ears. They had marveled as He cast away demons and fed thousands with a few loaves of bread and fish.

They had stood awe-stricken as Jesus spoke into the darkness of a tomb and called a dead man back to life. And now, standing in the middle of this strangely dark day, they watched as their faith ebbed away with each laboring breath of the Master.

> And when Jesus had cried with a loud voice, he said, Father, into thy hands I commend my spirit: and having said thus, he gave up the ghost.
>
> Luke 23:46

In that moment, all the disciples could think about was their despair. In the midst of their trouble all their minds could envision was danger, capture and the end of a dream. In those dark hours they did not recall the promise of Jesus. Neither did they consider the Scriptures that prophesied the very moment in which they lived.

Today, like the disciples, you may look around and see no reason for hope. You may even question the very notion of surviving your trial. But have you opened up the Scriptures, God's master plan for your life? Have you taken your eyes off your problem long enough to consider the promises of His holy Word?

> And I will bring the blind by a way that they knew not; I will lead them in paths that they have not known: I will make darkness light before them,

and crooked things straight. These things will I do unto them, and not forsake them.

Isaiah 42:16

Delight thyself also in the Lord; and he shall give thee the desires of thine heart.

Psalm 37:4

Had the disciples put aside their despair for a moment and delighted themselves in the words of Jesus, they would have remembered His promise to *rise on the third day*. Those three days of tribulation could have been a time of joy and preparation. Their moment of darkness could have been an occasion for *expectancy* — which is nothing more than good, old-fashioned faith.

Had they focused on God's promises instead of their problem, they would have known much sooner that it was not the end, but the beginning. Just as sure as their Jewish day began at sundown, they would have realized that mankind's new day had *already begun* — with the setting of the Son!

Though the disciples could not see it, a miracle was in motion: daylight was coming.

Nevertheless, thank God, there were a few who sought the Lord "while it was still dark." And those who did so were rewarded with a revelation they could never forget.

Early on the first day of the week, while it was still dark, Mary Magdalene went to the tomb and saw that the stone had been removed from the entrance. So she came running to Simon Peter and the other disciple, the one Jesus loved, and said, "They have

38

taken the Lord out of the tomb, and we don't know where they have put him!" (John)

So Peter and the other disciple (John) started for the tomb. Both were running, but the other disciple outran Peter and reached the tomb first. He bent over and looked in at the strips of linen lying there but did not go in. Then Simon Peter, who was behind him, arrived and went into the tomb. He saw the strips of linen lying there, as well as the burial cloth that had been around Jesus' head. The cloth was folded up by itself, separate from the linen. Finally the other disciple, who had reached the tomb first, also went inside. He saw and believed.

John 20:1-8 NIV

The tomb was empty. Tribulation was turned to triumph. The Son had risen. A new beginning had dawned in the dark. The morning light of God's divine grace shined on a new day for mankind.

There, at the world's *second* beginning, God gave us an example of how your trials can be conquered. He showed us that even when things look dark and it seems that nothing can be done, *then* is when your faith should be the strongest.

To God, your dark tomb of tribulation is just the fertile ground from which He will resurrect your deliverance. The instant you exercise your faith in His divine power, your tribulations turn into triumphs! My friend, when you put your trust in the very One Who created light, your darkest moments are just the beginning of a new day.

In your hour of despair, remember the promises of God's Word, and voice your expectancy in the face of darkness.

> And we have the word of the prophets made more certain, and you will do well to pay attention to it, as to a light shining in a dark place, until the day dawns and the morning star rises in your hearts.
>
> 2 Peter 1:19 NIV

Every morning the sun comes up, the Church needs to delight itself in the certainty of God's promises. We need to take our eyes off our problems and turn them toward Jesus, the Light of the world.

Certainty of Purpose

The tangible evidence of Christ's resurrection provided His shaken followers with a solid foundation rock of hope. His empty grave gave new life and meaning to Simon Peter's inspired confession, . . . **Thou art the Christ, the Son of the living God** (Matt. 16:16). On this *rock of revelation* the early Church was built.

That truth shored up the shaky structure of the disciples' faith and gave those first Christians something to live for . . . and die for. They were no longer afraid. *Their Master's promised resurrection turned their certain break up into a breakthrough of certainty.* Each one became a dynamo of faith and action. From Matthew to the apostle John, 11 individual instantaneous transformations took place.

On the day of Pentecost when these men and 108 others emerged from the upper room, they possessed an indisputable certainty of purpose. No longer would the disciples cower behind locked doors or deny involvement in the cause. Having a sure foundation of faith and the power of the Holy Spirit as their guide, these 12 resolved to allow no hardship, no tribulation, no threat of death to hinder them from proclaiming Jesus Christ as Savior, Lord and coming King!

Despite every test and torture, these men remained constant in their resolve. They kept their feet planted firmly on the Word, and their eyes fixed on the Prize.

According to John Foxe's thorough and revealing *Book of Martyrs,* each apostle demonstrated that "certainty" of purpose that propelled the early Church into action — and that same resolve is what we desperately need in the Church today.

The apostle James, the brother of John, the Revelator, was so adamant of his faith in Christ, that the very man who brought him to the court for sentencing was persuaded to become a Christian also. When the new convert publicly expressed his belief and asked for James's forgiveness, the apostle embraced him and gladly answered, "Peace be unto thee, brother." Eventually both men, being resolute in their conviction, calmly faced the executioner together, and were beheaded.

The apostle Thomas, who believed only after seeing the Master's nail scars with his own eyes, proclaimed that Good News throughout Persia and beyond. Without concern for his own life, he took the message of Christ eastward to India. There, tradition says that once-doubting Thomas declared his faith openly, up until the very day he was slain with a short spear.

Simon, the brother of Jude and James the younger, was a dynamic witness for the Son of God. For that reason he was crucified in Egypt.

Simon the apostle, called Zelotes, preached fervently throughout Africa; he was likewise crucified.

The apostle Mark, the first Bishop of Alexandria, passionately recounted the story and teachings of Jesus throughout Egypt. During the terrible reign of Trajan the emperor, the evangelist was dragged by ropes into a fire and left there to burn.

The disciple *Bartholomew* became a dedicated missionary to India, and is said to have translated the book of Matthew into that native dialect. Later in Armenia, he withstood numerous persecutions. He was finally beaten mercilessly with sticks, then crucified. Afterward he was beheaded.

Andrew, the brother of Peter, proclaimed the death and resurrection of Jesus Christ for close to 50 years. The disciple never shrank from his duty, no matter how hot the fires of persecution burned. Finally, after bringing many to the understanding of salvation, he confronted the governor of a large territory in what is now Ethiopia. He derided the ruler for worshipping idols and boldly declared the Son of God.

Being afraid of Andrew's growing influence with the people, the governor straightway ordered the disciple to be "fastened to the cross with all speed."

Matthew, Christ's disciple and author of the New Testament book that bears his name, diligently taught against the pagan practices of Ethiopia and Egypt. His straightforward ministry led many to the saving knowledge of God's Son. He was not ashamed to proclaim the gospel.

Upon realizing the threat of Matthew's liberating message, King Hircanus, the ruler of the area, sent a servant to the disciple — and ran him through with a spear.

Philip was a zealous messenger for Christ. Despite constant threats of mortal danger, he fearlessly declared the teachings of Jesus throughout the nations of the mideast. Tradition holds that after persevering through many trials, Philip was both crucified and stoned until dead.

James the just was a governor of the early Church. His example and his eloquence persuaded both Jews and Gentiles that Jesus of Nazareth was indeed the promised Messiah.

Noting the effect of this disciple's witness on the people, the scribes and Pharisees attempted to kill James by throwing him off a high place. However, instead of finding him dead, the Jewish leaders came upon him praying for their forgiveness.

It is said that as James sincerely prayed, he was struck in the head with an instrument commonly used to beat the dust from cloth. The disciple was buried where he fell.

From the soapbox sermon he preached on the day of Pentecost to the pastoral messages he declared to the early Church of Rome, *the apostle Peter* traveled this world testifying of the saving power of Jesus Christ.

Throughout his eventful ministry, he faced a multitude of adversity, including scourging, imprisonment and trials before kings. Ultimately, tradition states that Simon Peter suffered the agonizing torment of death on an upside-down cross. Yet through each abusing affliction, he boldly proclaimed his association to the One he once denied.

John, author of the New Testament Revelation, was among the youngest of the apostles, and the only one to live to a ripe old age. Tradition claims he lived nearly 100 years. This disciple dedicated his entire life to the declaration of Christ and the administering of His Church. However, he did not escape persecution.

In his long lifetime, John witnessed the miracle life, cruel death, and glorious resurrection of Jesus. He saw his Master's prophecy fulfilled with the destruction of Jerusalem. He could testify about the power of Pentecost and the resilience of the early Church.

John kept the faith, as one by one his fellow disciples met their death by the sword, the executioner's axe and the familiar cross. He persevered with his own dynamic ministry though he was opposed, over the years, by no fewer than 12 Roman emperors, among them Augustus and Nero.

In his old age, this "Son of Thunder" was banished by the emperor Domitian to the isle of Patmos. There, despite his desolate surroundings and seasoned body, he managed to maintain his spiritual walk to such a degree that Christ revealed to him the revelation of the end times. John's long-lasting testimony of faith never wavered.

These brave, dedicated men were committed, excited and sure of their faith. They built up the Church of Jesus Christ right in the middle of Satan's most ruthless attacks. They courageously looked death in the face and proclaimed the certainty of eternal life.

Just think what those mighty men of God could have accomplished utilizing the freedom the Church enjoys today. Our present world is nothing like those dangerous times. Sure, today's Church has had a few skirmishes with the government, but that's just red tape. The early Church had to deal with red blood.

Comparing our religious freedoms to that of the prophets and the early Church is like relating the delights of Disney World to the horrors of a World War II concentration camp.

The first Christians were committed to seeing lives transformed by the power of God, despite the personal dangers. Today, many so-called Christians complain when they have to drive to church in the rain!

Are you as committed to your faith as the disciples were? What if you were put into their dangerous position? Would you cower in a locked room? Or would you take a stand for Christ — even if it meant your life?

If you don't stand for something, you'll fall for anything. If we, the Church, fail to wake out of our complacency and neglect to shore up our spiritual foundation, those long-gone days of persecution will once again shake us from our sleep. If we don't start caring about the world that exists outside the safety of our church walls, the tremors of the shaking will reverberate our structure down to a useless pile of rubble.

Our time is short. The needle of the Richter scale is fluttering. Like Shadrach, Meshach and Abednego, only those who are willing to go through the fires of tribulation will survive the heat. God is coming for a Church that is strong. He is still looking for a stubborn select few.

> . . . And [the Lord] called to the man clothed with linen, who had the writer's ink bottle at his side.
>
> And the Lord said to him, *Go through the midst of the city, through the midst of Jerusalem, and set a mark upon the foreheads of the men who sigh and groan over all the abominations that are committed in the midst of it.*
>
> And to the others He said in my hearing. Follow [the man with the ink bottle] through the city, and *smite; let not your eye spare, neither have any pity.*
>
> *Slay outright* the elderly, the young man and the virgin, the infant and the women; *but do not touch or go near any one on whom is the mark. Begin at My sanctuary.*
>
> Ezekiel 9:3-6 AMP

Back in Ezekiel's day, God began his search in the Church. He never changes. That's where He is looking now. If the Lord walked down the aisle of His sanctuary today, would he find you there? Would he place His mark on you?

His Church was built by men and women who saw the dark abominations of their world and did something about them — even at the cost their lives. The adversities that the early Church went through made their faith strong. How do today's adversities affect your convictions?

Do you possess the kind of faith to stand firm no matter how dark things may seem? Are you willing to step on a few toes, and even stick your neck out?

The Church of today must be willing to go through anything and yield to nothing except God's will. If we are going to survive the shaking, we have to get back to our roots — back to the perseverance of the prophets and the unselfish commitment of the early Church.

It is imperative that we be willing and ready to walk through the fire for Christ Jesus. It's time we shored up our foundation and acquired God's special mark of "certainty."

Like those who have gone before us, if we are to *survive* the heat, we must be prepared to walk *through* the fire.

The Long-Distance Runner

"If you're going through a problem,
that means you've got momentum.
You are *going* through!"

CHAPTER
III

. . . in labours more abundant, in stripes above measure, in prisons more frequent, in deaths oft.

Of the Jews five times received I forty stripes save one.

Thrice was I beaten with rods, once was I stoned, thrice I suffered shipwreck, a night and a day I have been in the deep;

In journeyings often, in perils of waters, in perils of robbers, in perils by mine own countrymen, in perils by the heathen, in perils in the city, in perils in the wilderness, in perils in the sea, in perils among false brethren;

In weariness and painfulness, in watchings often, in hunger and thirst, in fastings often, in cold and nakedness.

2 Corinthians 11: 23-27

Upon reading this passage from one of Paul's letters to the church of Corinth, you might be inclined to think that the old apostle was complaining. If so, you would be badly mistaken. He was not complaining — he was bragging.

This man, who once served as the chief prosecutor of the early Church, was now looking back on his transformed life, recalling the old war stories of survival. Paul was, in effect, encouraging his fellow Christians to "keep on keepin' on."

Today, the Church needs to hear this same message. We have to learn how to turn tribulation into triumph.

Paul described in eloquent detail how he suffered through incredible hardships and experiences that would have broken a weaker will. Yet he endured them all with an enduring faith that allowed him to emerge not only victorious, but stronger.

Yes, tribulations are draining physically, mentally and spiritually; nevertheless, God does not leave us ill-equipped for the battle.

> For no temptation [no trial regarded as enticing to sin, no matter how it comes or where it leads] — has overtaken you and laid hold on you that is not common to man — that is, no temptation or trial has come to you that is beyond human resistance and that is not adjusted and adapted and belonging to human experience, and such as man can bear. But God is faithful [to His Word and to His compassionate nature], and He [can be trusted] not to let you be tempted and tried and assayed beyond your ability and strength of resistance and power to endure, but with the temptation He will [always] also provide the way out — the means of escape to a landing place

— that you may be capable and strong and powerful patiently to bear up under it.

1 Corinthians 10:13 AMP

God is our refuge and strength, a very present help in trouble.

Psalms 46:1

Instead of looking at the physical and whining, "Woe is me," we must learn how to tap into God's spiritual arsenal and wear the devil out. If we can mirror Paul's example of endurance and place our confidence in the strong hands of God, we can turn our every "woe" into "winnings."

Paul said that many doors were opened to him, but none without great tribulation. (2 Cor. 11:23-28.) Those who think that we are here to breeze through life had better stop and think again. We are not placed in this world to attend a perpetual praise and worship service — that comes later. We are here to experience, learn, grow and teach.

Our job is to learn not only *of* God, but also *from* God, that we might tell others *about* God, so all men can be drawn closer *to* God.

Yet, as we have already read, those who preach the truth are not usually found on top of the world's most-wanted list. Those who follow the leading of the Spirit repulse society. If we, the Church of today, are to bear witness to the Gospel, we will most assuredly be oppressed by Satan like the prophets and early Christians. However, if we are sensitive to the Spirit, *God can use even these times of trial as an opportunity to both learn and teach.*

If you are thrown into prison, don't complain, but remember Paul and Silas. (Acts 16.) Let the others in that cell know that there is something *different* about you.

Your reactions to the devil's opposition are important. They can strengthen your spiritual foundation and point others to Christ.

If we want to get the world's attention, we must, like Paul, believe and practice what we preach. The apostle put it this way:

> But watch thou in all things, *endure afflictions, do the work* of an evangelist, *make full proof* of thy ministry.
>
> 2 Timothy 4:5

What it all boils down to is *endurance;* the ability to tolerate a situation with patience, stamina and determination.

Spiritual Stamina

In Galatians there is a list that describes the attributes of a good Christian. In that roster one characteristic stands out: *long-suffering.* This word implies "a drawn-out ordeal," which is by all accounts a description of tribulation.

It is this rare ability to suffer long which fosters the perfection of endurance. This spiritual stamina gives one the skill to remain calm in the face of frustration. It keeps you from losing your temper. Long-suffering can unclench a fist.

How many times have you been angry at God? I remember when seven members of my family died within eighteen months. I lost my 17-year-old cousin to Hodgkin's disease, then my uncle came back from Viet Nam in a body bag. He had a beautiful face and a melodic voice — all snuffed out in the prime of life. I remember when mother got the news. She grabbed her hair, ran through the house and out into the street screaming at God. Back then we didn't have the revelation that we do now.

I have learned, through the spiritual perspective of long-suffering, that no matter how the devil shuffles the cards, God always has the winning hand. Despite what we may face today or tomorrow, we can be assured that the ability of God on the inside of us is sufficient to remedy every situation.

Sorrow, disappointment and self-pity are the hurdles Satan sets up along the course of our life. And the main attribute of long-suffering is the spiritual stamina that enables us to *consistently clear* those obstacles.

Refuse To Quit

Even if someone comes to an altar, gives his life to Jesus and starts the race, he is not guaranteed the prize. Not everyone that shoots out of the starting blocks will wear the winner's wreath.

> **But he that shall endure unto the end, the same shall be saved.**
>
> Matthew 24:13

To those who persevere, there is nothing big enough, bad enough or ugly enough to separate them from the love of God.

> For I am persuaded beyond doubt — am sure
> — that neither death nor life, nor angels nor
> principalities, nor things impending and threatening
> nor things to come, nor powers,
>
> Nor height nor depth, nor anything else in all
> creation will be able to separate us from the love of
> God which is in Christ Jesus our Lord.
>
> Romans 8:38,39 AMP

Only those with faith and resilience will cross the finish line. Like the tenacious apostle Paul, I too want to brag one day. It is the goal of my life to possess the durability to run the entire race. It is the desire of my soul to finish the course. I am determined to endure till the end.

I pray that the Holy Spirit will produce in me the heart of a long-distance runner. I don't want to start strong and gradually lose momentum along the way. I want to maintain a steady pace and cross the finish line with my eyes on the Prize.

The course so far has had its hindrances, and there have been times that the enemy has quickened the pace to tire me out. The sweat has poured down my back, my legs have burned and there have been moments when my lungs felt like they would explode. But praise God! I'm still on my feet!

Long-suffering enables you to ignore your surroundings and your physical feelings. It keeps your eyes focused on the Prize which the Bible calls the mark of the high calling of God.

However, some Christians live as if the race they are running is just a short Sunday afternoon sprint. These "joggers" assume that they will never get a cramp or strain a muscle. And if they happen to come across an obstacle in their path, they immediately panic.

Personally, I need a double dose of long-suffering every time I see one of these touchy "Christians." If someone steps on their toes, they're ready to quit the race. If some preacher they idolize falls in disgrace, they throw up their hands and walk off the track.

At the first sign of perspiration, these weak-kneed complainers wipe their brow and grumble, "No one understands what I'm going through!" They think that a little spiritual sweat is a sure sign that they are *not* going to make it.

If they allow that kind of negative, physical-minded thinking to take hold, *then they are right! They won't make it!*

What they don't seem to understand is that spiritual perspiration is a good indication that you're making advancement toward the Prize. If you're "going through" a problem, that means you've got momentum! You ARE *going through!*

When the hurdles of sorrow, temptation, despair and distress loom in front of you, the virtue of long-suffering will provide you with the *spiritual stamina* to rise above it all. God has not called His Church to do anything that He has not given us the strength to finish.

Adversity makes the strong *stronger!* It's time for the Church to start exercising its faith and quit complaining.

When the prophet Jeremiah started murmuring about the rough road, God told him that if running with footmen had wearied him, how could he contend with horses? (Jer. 12:5.) Likewise, if we can't handle the little things life throws in our path, how do we expect to contend with Satan's treachery? The answer is simple — *Jesus!*

God's only Son was no stranger to tribulation. In fact, the prophet Isaiah referred to Him as a "man of sorrows...acquainted with grief." Looking through the Holy Spirit's telescope of time, the prophet described in vivid detail a trial that no mere man could survive:

> But he was wounded for our transgressions, he was bruised for our iniquities: the chastisement of our peace was upon him; and with his stripes we are healed...and the Lord hath laid upon him the iniquity of us all.
>
> Isaiah 53:5,6

Some 700 years after Isaiah spoke these words, a Roman whip tore into the flesh of Jesus Christ's back. With each bloodletting incision, the Son of God bore upon Himself the nauseating agony of every disease that mankind would ever know. He suffered long through the intense torment of those 39 lashes so that we could proclaim, "By His stripes we were healed."

Led by His tormentors up the steep incline of Golgotha's hill, He was made to lie down on the long beam of the cross forcing the raw, open wounds of His back against the rough, splintery wood. The pain must have been excruciating.

Then without warning, there came the sudden bone-shaking thud of a hammer. The nails that were pounded into His hands and feet that day "injected" Him with every blatant iniquity, every subtle sin, every vile act that mankind had ever or would ever commit.

". . . The Lord hath laid upon Him the iniquity of us all."

Jesus Christ became our substitute. He suffered long and died in our place. He endured the peril of Calvary so we wouldn't have to suffer. By simply believing in His substitutionary gift and the miracle of His resurrection, we can be cleansed from our unrighteousness, healed of every manner of sickness, and overcome any obstacle that Satan throws in our path!

He went the distance. Jesus ran the ultimate obstacle course of tribulations and emerged the winner. He withstood Satan's best shot and even outlived death itself.

He could have called an army of angels, yet He willingly stayed on the cross. *He came through the most torturous of tribulations and triumphed!* So what do we have to fear? He has already won the battle!

The apostle John said that our faith in what Christ has already accomplished is the victory that overcomes the world. (1 John 5:4.) The reward of that divine accomplishment is what awaits us just across the finish line.

If we are going to break the tape on the course that Paul championed, we must maintain the persistence of a long-distance, long-suffering runner, and never give up!

Christ suffered and gave His best for His Church. Isn't it time for His Church to do its best for Him? Let's get our eyes off the physical and concentrate on the Holy Spirit's leading.

Let's remember why we are here:

1. To learn OF God through our daily walk in the Spirit;

2. To gain strength FROM God through the trials and tests along the way;

3. To be an example that testifies ABOUT God, and;

4. To draw all men TO God.

Rather than complaining, if we will persevere, and acquire the heart of a long-distance runner, then one of these days we can all sit around the throne with our family and friends and swap war stories with Paul.

. . . and that's something to brag about.

TRIBULATION
TO TRIUMPH

PART
Two

"...To win we have to be smart."

Turn the Tables on Trouble

"Being wise as a serpent
is not necessarily a bad thing."

CHAPTER
IV

As I sat and watched the aftermath of the San Francisco earthquake, I couldn't help but notice how carefully the rescue teams went about their work. Although every second counted, they did not rush headlong into burning, crumbling buildings. They wisely evaluated the affected area and considered every potential danger — before they acted.

Thanks to their preparatory training and in-the-field experience, these professionals knew exactly what precautions to take. They were aware that one wrong move could capsize a shaky wall. They knew that one misplaced step could collapse a weakened floor. Rushing into an unchecked room filled with leaking gas could easily set off a spark. And charging through a debris-littered street could very well lead to contact with an exposed live wire.

These brave men and women were ready and willing to risk their lives to save others, but in the handling of that mission, they were *not* foolhardy. In the middle of that mass destruction, panic and chaos, they displayed an impressive application of good old-fashioned *wisdom*. Oh, how I wish that I could say the same for the Church of today!

Now, more than at any other time in history, the Church of Jesus Christ needs to be a willing and discerning participant in the rescue of mankind. We have the Answer. We possess the means of escaping this disastrous world before all hell breaks loose. But some of us are not quite sure of how to go about it.

Every Sunday from America's pulpits, ministers deliver lofty sermons and use such eloquent theology that only a seminary professor could understand them. And on those rare occasions when we do step outside the church walls, that "pointing finger" message we often zealously declare, usually chases away the very wounded victims that need God's touch. To effectively save the world, we have to use wisdom.

Five-dollar words may impress an audience, but the simple Word of God is what they need.

> For the Word that God speaks is alive and full of power — making it active, operative, energizing and effective; it is sharper than any two-edged sword, penetrating to the dividing line of the breath of life (soul) and [the immortal] spirit, and of joints and marrow, [of the deepest parts of our nature], exposing and sifting and analyzing and judging the very thoughts and purposes of the heart.
>
> Hebrews 4:12 AMP

When we go out into the debris-strewn streets to rescue the lost, we have to learn how to evaluate the surroundings first, lest we make a wrong move and capsize a shaky soul. Although the Church has brave men and women willing to risk the tribulations of hell to salvage the lost, it is imperative that we learn how to handle that important mission — competently.

We are in a war. To survive, we must be strong. To win, we must be *smart*.

Playing the Devil's Game

Jesus Christ understood the importance of wisdom better than anyone. As a matter of fact, He felt that it was so vital to the mission of the church, that He made it a basic requirement:

> Lo, I am sending you out like sheep in the midst of wolves: be wary and wise as serpents, and be innocent (harmless, guileless and without falsity) as doves.
>
> And you will be brought before governors and kings for My sake, for a witness to bear testimony before them and to the Gentiles (the nations).
>
> But when they deliver you up, do not be anxious about how or what you are to speak; for what you are to say will be given you in that very hour and moment.
>
> Matthew 10:16,18,19 AMP

When Christ spoke these words, He was giving his twelve disciples a final piece of advice before sending them out into the world for the first time. In effect, He was telling them, "Don't let the devil pull the wool over your eyes." But at the same time He also implied, "Don't worry about what to do or say, because the things I have taught you will come to your mind and, . . . it shall be given you in that same hour what you shall speak."

Being wise as a serpent is not necessarily a bad thing. The wisdom to which Jesus was referring in this passage is *craftiness*. It is being *shrewd* and *subtle*. It is staying sharp and on your toes. It's knowing what to do and what to say at the proper time to successfully reach a given objective. In this case the objective is proclaiming the Gospel to the world.

Christ's analogy of a serpent's "crafty" wisdom is no doubt in reference to Genesis 3 where Satan came to Eve in a unique serpent-like form. In fact, the word Jesus used for "wise" is ironically the *same* Greek word used to describe Satan's serpent-like behavior in the garden. There with all of his shrewd skill, he slyly lured Eve toward destruction.

> Now the serpent was more *subtle* than any other wild creature that the Lord God had made. He said to the woman, "Did God say, 'You shall not eat of any tree in the garden'?" And the women said to the serpent, "We may eat of the fruit of the trees of the garden, but God said, 'You shall not eat of the fruit of the tree which is in the midst of the garden, neither shall you touch it, lest you die.' "

> But the serpent said to the woman, "You will not die. For God knows that when you eat of it your eyes

will be opened, and you will be like God, knowing good and evil."

So when the woman saw that the tree was good for food, and that it was a delight to the eyes...she took of its fruit and ate; and she also gave some to her husband, and he ate.

Then the Lord God said unto the woman, "What is this that you have done?" The woman said, "The serpent beguiled me, and I ate."

Genesis 3:1-6,13 RSV

In this instance the word "subtle" is not a description of the way the serpent moved, but rather the way the devil "inside" the serpent *thought*. Out of jealousy, Satan wanted to put a wedge between God and His creation. Finding Eve alone, he seized the opportunity, and *subtly* pointed out to her the advantages of eating the forbidden fruit (duly noting that she would become "like God"). This shrewd, enticing notion was all he needed to push her and the rest of mankind right over the edge.

The devil knew just *what* to say and *when* to say it to accomplish *exactly* what he wanted. And, as strange as it might seem, on that day when Jesus sent out His twelve disciples, His advice to them was to be just as cunning and "serpent-like."

By telling them to be "as wise as serpents," Christ was, in effect, saying that *they* could *turn the tables on Satan* by using the devil's own tricks! And in doing so, they could accomplish exactly what God had wanted, ever since that fateful day in the garden — to be reconciled with man through the instruction and knowledge of His Son.

It is the Almighty's desire for us,

> To know wisdom and instruction; to perceive the words of understanding;
>
> To receive the instruction of wisdom, justice and judgment and equity.
>
> To give subtlety to the simple, to the young man knowledge and discretion.
>
> Proverbs 1:2-4

If a Christian truly possesses prudence, his mind is tirelessly at work devising *practical ways* to reach his goal. He is alert, and constantly on his toes, looking for any opening to advance his course, which is the Gospel of Jesus Christ.

Therefore, if the Church is commanded to use wisdom to beat the devil at his own game, it is important that we understand what wisdom is and how it works.

The Origin of Wisdom

Before the stars twinkled, before the moon cast its blue-white glow upon the earth, even before the concept of time came into being, wisdom existed. As a matter of fact, this incredible power was not only present at the beginning, it was the very tool God wielded to bring about creation itself.

> The Lord by wisdom hath founded the earth; by understanding hath he established the heavens.

> By his knowledge the depths are broken up, and
> the clouds drop down the dew.
>
> Proverbs 3:19,20

Yes, the Lord, himself formed this world by merely *thinking* it into existence. By His divine *spoken thoughts* earth awoke, opened its sleepy eyes and rumbled to life. Just think of it; God's powerful words, charged with WISDOM, echoed out through the heavens, and, in its audible wake, planets, stars, and galaxies were formed without number.

> And God said, Let there be light... And God
> said, Let there be a firmament in the midst of the
> waters...And God said, Let the earth bring forth
> grass... And God said, Let there be lights in the
> firmament of the heaven to divide the day from
> night... And God said, Let us make man in our
> image...
>
> Genesis 1:3,6,11,14,26

Over the centuries, wisdom has assisted both God and His creation, man, in countless inventive endeavors. However, the source of wisdom's strength is not contained within itself. Like a paintbrush cradled in the hands of an artist, the power of this tool lies within the discretion of the creator.

God *is* the originator of wisdom. He is the One and the only source of its spiritual power. The apostle Paul put it this way:

> O the depth of the riches both of the *wisdom* and
> *knowledge* of God! how unsearchable are his
> judgments, and his ways past finding out!

> For who hath known the mind of the Lord? or
> who hath been his counsellor?
>
> For *of* him, and *through* him, and *to* him, *are* all
> things: to whom be glory forever. Amen.
>
> Romans 11:33,34,36

Although it is an awesome force, the existence of
wisdom would mean very little to us if it were just an
unattainable power written about in the scriptures. But
thank God, it is so much more! For the Lord is not only
the *source* of all wisdom and knowledge, he is also the *supplier*
and the *only distributor* of this grand *gift!*

To *all* who will simply *ask,* God promises in James
1:5 that wisdom *shall* be given.

> If any of you lack wisdom, let him ask of God,
> that giveth to all men liberally, and upbraideth not;
> and it shall be given him.
>
> James 1:5

The foolhardy who rely on their own ingenuity live
under a dangerous liability. Without God's wisdom, the
hurdles of tribulation are higher and its ditches are deeper.
Without wisdom we are virtually defenseless against the
sneaky, subtle pitfalls of Satan.

The gift of God's understanding opens the eyes,
sharpens the intellect and gives us the ability to create "witty
inventions" (Prov. 8:12) to confuse Satan's inferior plans.
Only by God's wisdom can we truly triumph over
tribulation.

Wisdom is not just a simple collection of knowledge.
It is three separate, yet combined, forces that work in close

harmony with the three basic functions of man: spirit, soul, and body. Through this unique interaction, the full impact of God's understanding can be realized.

SOPHIA:
The Gift of Rare Insight

"... When that key turned, Bezaleel began to 'realize'
Much more than he actually 'knew.'"

CHAPTER
V

The first of wisdom's powerful facets is *Sophia* which is Greek for skill, cleverness and learning.* This form of understanding influences the spiritual side of man's intellect. It deals particularly with the gift of rare insight. Sophia allows one to comprehend new ideas, create and implement new concepts, and gain a special understanding of God's ultimate things.

Proverbs refers to this attribute this way:

> I wisdom dwell with prudence and find out knowledge of witty inventions.
>
> Proverbs 8:12

This spiritual side of wisdom is not only capable of providing cunning ways to accomplish insurmountable tasks, it is also able to open up the supernatural eyes of

---

*Definitions in this chapter and the following chapters are based on definitions in *Hebrew/Greek Keys Study Bible*, Spiros Zodhiates, editor. (Grand Rapids: Baker Book House, 1984.)

those who are willing, so that God can reveal to them His ultimate plan for their lives. "The wisdom of the prudent," Proverbs 14:8 states, "is to understand his way."

All too often the Lord's divine purposes and goals for us are so high above our "normal" thinking that they seem impossible to reach. Still, for those who voluntarily open up their hearts and minds to His plans, no matter how difficult the task, God will "liberally" impart to them both the vision and the *sophia*-knowledge necessary to reach their goal.

We *must* learn to submit ourselves totally to the Spirit. Opening up ourselves to His will is to simply:

> Trust in the Lord with all thine heart; and lean not unto thine own understanding.
>
> In all thy ways acknowledge him, and he shall direct thy paths.
>
> Proverbs 3:5-6

A Tool in the Desert

Beneath the clouds that engulfed the slopes of Mount Sinai, Moses reverently listened while God Himself laid out His plans for His chosen people. During the course of this once-in-a-lifetime conversation, God chronicled for Moses the strict guidelines He had imposed upon the Israelites. Among these rules, the Lord revealed that His people were to ". . . keep the Sabbath day," and worship Him and Him alone in a *tabernacle* of His own divine design (Ex. 20:10.)

The Lord instructed Moses that this tent-like structure was to be made of a particular material and dimension, and that its interior was to be filled with specifically proportioned furniture and accessories. Everything from golden candlesticks to special clothing was to be created for this most important and holy place.

It was obvious that God expected the children of Israel to pause on their journey, gather up their resources and actually construct a "church" for Him in the middle of the wilderness.

With their limited supplies, how could these nomadic people accomplish such an enormous task? Even under the most civilized of conditions a job of this magnitude would be a challenge. But to start a building program in the middle of a desert? It seemed impossible.

Nevertheless, as surely as God has a plan and a design, it is certain that He also has a prepared man in mind:

And the Lord spake unto Moses saying,

See I have called by name *Bezaleel,* the son of Uri, the son of Hur, of the tribe of Judah:

And I have filled him with the spirit of God, in wisdom, and in understanding, and in knowledge, and in all manner of workmanship,

To devise cunning works, to work in gold, and in silver, and in brass,

And in cutting of stones, to set them, and in carving of timber to work all manner of workmanship.

73

And I, behold, I have given with him Aholiab, the son of Ahisamach of the tribe of Dan: *and in the hearts of all that are wise hearted I have put wisdom,* that they may make all that I have commanded thee;

The tabernacle of the congregation, and the ark of the testimony, and the mercy seat that is thereupon, and all the furniture of the tabernacle,

And the table and his furniture, and the pure candlestick with all his furniture, and the altar of incense,

And the altar of burnt offering with all his furniture, and the laver and his foot,

And the cloths of service and the holy garments for Aaron the priest, and the garments of his sons to minister in the priest's office.

And the anointing oil, and the sweet incense for the holy place: according to all that I have commanded thee shall they do.

Exodus 31:1-11

No doubt, Bezaleel was already a master craftsman. Born a Jewish slave, he most likely learned his profession under the sting of a task master's whip. Almost certainly he had hammered and chiseled for many years, dangling like a modern-day window washer along the walls of Pharaoh's well-crafted shrines.

Those long years of intense hands-on training are what actually *prepared* Bezaleel for his task. Ironically that body of stored-up learning was just the "input" he needed to ready himself for the plan God had for his life.

Upon submitting himself to the divine plan (for God never forces His will on anyone), he became, overnight, the most valuable man in the camp. He became, in effect, God's tool in the wilderness.

On that rumbling mountain, when the Lord told Moses that He had "filled" Bezaleel . . . **with the spirit of God, in wisdom, and in understanding, and in knowledge, and in all manner of workmanship. . . (Ex. 31:3).** The Almighty had in fact switched on wisdom, and charged the craftsman's spirit mind with the skill and the cleverness of *Sophia* knowledge.

To put it simply, when that key turned, Bezaleel began to "realize" much more than he actually "knew." His capacity to "devise cunning works" rapidly expanded. And eventually his wise *"output"* was able to answer all the impossible questions of building a church in the desert.

Likewise, we need to get into the Spirit and discover what God's plan is for our personal lives so that we can be better prepared to build up the Church today. As a result of his acquired knowledge, Israel was provided with a cunningly crafted "mobile" tabernacle in which they could worship God through their long desert journey. Thanks to that acquired wisdom, Bezaleel is remembered in the Scriptures for his creative handiwork and skillful supervision.

This master craftsman was able to realize and fulfill the purpose for his life because he was both *ready* and *willing* to work for God. He acquired the necessary knowledge he needed *first.* Then, he willingly accepted

God's gift of *Sophia*-wisdom to make that stored-up knowledge work to his advantage.

This divine facet of understanding sparks spiritual insight. It not only opens the mind to the same creative power that "thought" the world into existence; it can, as well, enlighten every committed Christian with the proper knowledge to rescue the world and expand the Church of Jesus Christ.

Like the star which guided the wise men, *Sophia*-wisdom can light your way. It can guide you through every snare of Satan. No matter how high your hurdles may be, the tool of *Sophia*-wisdom is able to build in you a tabernacle of spiritual understanding. And through that gift of rare insight, you can discover, for yourself, the same Source of knowledge that the wise men ultimately found — the wisdom of Jesus.

PHRONESIS:
The Power of Small Details

"God has placed in each of us a mind
to rationalize out everyday situations."

CHAPTER
VI

The second of wisdom's attributes is *Phronesis*. In the Greek, the word denotes understanding, attitude and practical wisdom. This facet of knowledge centers its influence on the *soul* or the conscience mind of man. It deals with the *practical, ordinary things* that shape our daily lives.

If *Sophia* reveals the footpath to one's ultimate goal, then *Phronesis* tells you the proper shoes to wear for the journey.

This kind of practical wisdom is found throughout the book of Proverbs. Though the truths are simple and plainly put, each verse is packed with the very essence of *Phronesis* — common sense.

> Whoso keepeth his mouth and his tongue keepeth his soul from troubles.
>
> Proverbs 21:23

The simple (man) believeth every word: but the prudent man looketh well to his going.

Proverbs 14:15

The poor is hated even of his own neighbour: but the rich hath many friends.

Proverbs 14:20

Yet a little sleep, a little slumber, a little folding of the hands to sleep:

So shall thy poverty come as one that travelleth; and thy want as an armed man.

Proverbs 24:33,34

Although these teachings are short and to the point, their lessons are nonetheless profound. Such are the subtle ways of *Phronesis,* the wisdom of small, yet important details.

This attribute does not concern itself with the "big picture," but rather focuses on the subtle shades, colors and brush strokes that make up the entire painting. *Phronesis* is understanding how to take care of life's small problems, so that they do not grow to be major difficulties. One unique individual who exhibited this form of wisdom admirably was that committed young Christian, Stephen.

During the tribulations of the early Church, the apostles were busily preaching and teaching the message of Jesus Christ to all who would listen. It was a 24-hour-a-day job, and by its nature, evangelizing the world left little time for the apostles to deal with life's small details. However, one particular issue eventually grew to the point where it *had* to be addressed.

> And in those days, when the number of the
> disciples was multiplied, there arose a murmuring of
> the Grecians against the Hebrews because their
> widows were neglected in the daily ministration.
>
> Acts 6:1

In the great scheme of things, it was a little problem, but important nonetheless. What kind of Christian example would the early Church have displayed if its leaders ignored the needs of those within their reach? What kind of message would it send to an already skeptical world if they preached, "I come that you might have life," and then allowed their own widows to go hungry and die? Something had to be done. But what?

> Then the twelve called the multitude of the
> disciples unto them, and said, It is not reason that we
> should leave the word of God and serve tables.
>
> Acts 6:2

Plainly put, the apostles were saying, "We don't have time to handle this; we are Christ's messengers to the world, not waiters in a restaurant." It was a simple, yet complex situation. This problem had to be resolved quickly, without hindering the growing momentum of the Church's evangelistic strides. Obviously a *practical* approach was needed. And with that in mind, a solution was ultimately proposed.

> Wherefore, brethren, look ye out among you
> seven men of honest report, full of the Holy Ghost
> and wisdom, whom we may appoint over this
> business.

> But we (the twelve) will give ourselves continually
> to prayer, and to the ministry of the word.
>
> Acts 6:3,4

To be one of seven chosen out of that large body says a lot about Stephen. He, no doubt, had already proven himself to be a responsible and practical man. And, most assuredly, the *Phronesis* wisdom he exhibited in procuring and distributing necessities to those Grecian widows added to his standing in the Christian community. In a short span of time, Stephen showed himself to be a man greatly used of God.

> And Stephen, full of faith and power, did great
> wonders and miracles among the people.
>
> Acts 6:8

In fact, his influence became so great that Satan's forces were determined to trip him up.

> Then there arose certain of the synagogue, which
> is called the synagogue of the Libertines, and
> Cyrenians, and Alexandrians, and of them of Cilicia
> and of Asia, disputing with Stephen.
>
> Acts 6:9

These great diversified minds of this international theological body, came down hard upon Stephen with all of their collective fervor and knowledge. Still, this young man won the day by rebutting them with the *common* sense of his conscious mind and with *practical illustrations* of his dynamic faith in God.

> And they were not able to resist the (Phronesis)
> wisdom and the spirit by which he spake.
>
> Acts 6:10

Stephen's *Sophia*-understanding of the Lord's power placed him on the road to God's ultimate plan for his life. His *Phronesis*-knowledge of practical things helped him to *confound* the theological minds of his age. This second facet of wisdom gave Stephen the common sense and divine logic to confuse Satan's ploys. Though he eventually became Christianity's first martyr, his wise example helped to give the early Church the practical attitude and the solid, common sense foundation it needed to flourish.

Phronesis is logic and proficiency. As Jesus once illustrated in Luke 14:29,30, this form of wisdom can be likened to a man who sits down and counts the cost *before* he decides to build a house:

> . . . lest haply, after he hath laid the foundation, and is not able to finish it, all that behold it begin to mock him,
>
> Saying, this man began to build, and was not able to finish.

To "count the cost" is obviously a wise act, but there are many Christians walking our streets today who can't even muster the discipline to stay within their household budget. No matter how much income they earn, they always manage — or should I say *mis*manage — to overspend!

As Christians, we should demonstrate self-control in all things. We must be disciplined, which is to apply a practical attitude toward a specific area of life. *Phronesis*, defined in the Greek, is practical wisdom. It speaks to the conscious mind. This department of wisdom is capable of developing the discipline and self-control we need. By its nature, *Phronesis* is not flighty or frivolous, but rather subtle and restrained.

Take, for instance, the Old Testament account of Nabal and his wife Abigail. Their contrasting qualities of wisdom and frivolity are prime examples of what we should seek after — and avoid.

> Now the name of the man was Nabal; and the name of his wife Abigail: and she was a woman of good understanding, and of a beautiful countenance: but the man was churlish and evil in his doings; and he was of the house of Caleb.
>
> 1 Samuel 25:3

In his day, Nabal was considered to be a wealthy man owning three thousand sheep and a thousand goats. It so happened, in this episode, that his large flocks were in Carmel, near to where David camped out in hiding from Saul.

As a courtesy to this wealthy man, David and his men kept a protective eye on both Nabal's shepherds and his flocks. They saw to it that neither harm nor a loss of livestock occurred during their watch.

Later, learning that Nabal was in Carmel for the shearing of his flocks, David sent ten young men to greet him and to request a return of his courtesy in the form of food for his camp. However, the rich man's reply was a far cry from what Israel's future king expected:

> And Nabal answered David's servants, and said, Who is David? and who is the son of Jesse? there be

> many servants nowadays that break away every man from his master.
>
> Shall I then take my bread, and my water, and my flesh that I have killed for my shearers, and give it unto men, whom I know not whence they be?
>
> And David said unto his men, Gird ye on every man his sword. And they girded on every man his sword; and David also girded on his sword: and there went up after David about four hundred men...
>
> 1 Samuel 25:10-11,13

Though Nabal had wealth and a degree of power, he lacked the wisdom to see that this seemingly small matter of turning away a few young men was about to explode into a life-threatening problem. His attitude was carefree, flighty and frivolous. He could not see the simple common sense of repaying courtesy for courtesy. And in this selfish stupor, Nabal was oblivious to the strength of David's wrath and approaching army.

> But one of the young men told Abigail, Nabal's wife saying, Behold, David sent messengers out of the wilderness to salute our master; and he (Nabal) railed on them...now therefore know and consider what thou wilt do; for evil is determined against our master, and against all his household: for he is such a son of Belial, that a man cannot speak to him.
>
> 1 Samuel 25:14,17

For this brave servant to speak so bluntly about his master's demeanor to the master's wife, is proof indeed that Nabal was a hateful man. But what of Abigail, this woman of "good understanding?"

Then Abigail made haste, and took two hundred loaves, and two bottles of wine, and five sheep ready dressed, and five measures of parched corn, and an hundred clusters of raisins, and two hundred cakes of figs, and laid them on asses.

And she said unto her servants, Go on before me; behold, I come after you. But she told not her husband Nabal.

1 Samuel 25:18,19

Abigail was indeed a wise woman. The *Phronesis* placed in her by God allowed her to both see the volatile nature of the situation and devise a rational plan to avoid it. Note how she handles her confrontation with David.

When Abigail saw David, she made haste, and alighted from the ass, and fell before David on her face... "Upon me alone, my lord, be the guilt; pray let your handmaid speak in your ears...Let not my lord regard the ill-natured fellow, Nabal; for as his name is, so is he; Nabal is his name, and folly is with him; but I your handmaid did not see the young men... whom you sent.

Now then... seeing the Lord has restrained you from bloodguilt, and from taking vengeance with your own hand, now then let your enemies and those who seek to do evil to my lord be as Nabal. And now let this present which your servant has brought to my lord be given to the young men who follow my lord."

1 Samuel 25:23-27 RSV

On her knees at David's feet, Abigail goes on to say,

"And when the Lord has done to my lord according to all the good that he has spoken concerning you, and has appointed you prince over Israel, my lord shall have no cause of grief, or pangs of conscience, for having shed blood without cause or for my lord taking vengeance himself"...

And David said to Abigail, "Blessed be the Lord, the God of Israel, who sent you to meet me! *Blessed be your discretion* and blessed be you, who have kept me this day from bloodguilt and from avenging myself with my own hand...unless you had made haste and come to meet me, truly by morning there had not been left to Nabal so much as one male."

Then David received from her hand what she had brought him; and he said to her, "Go up in peace to your house; see, I have hearkened to your voice, and I have granted your petition."

1 Samuel 25:30-35 RSV

Abigail was able to defuse this potentially volatile situation by using what David called "discretion," which is just another word for wisdom. First, she brought the food which David requested (fulfilling Nabal's responsibility) and she placed the blame of the entire affair on herself — promoting sympathy. Then Abigail said that her husband (the object of David's rage) was nothing more than a man of "folly," which in effect made Nabal uninteresting and unworthy of David's attention.

Finally, she put in David's mind the truthful notion that vengeance is the Lord's prerogative, and that he would eventually regret his planned violent reprisal. Most certainly Abigail had learned the lesson of Proverbs 1:33:

> Whosoever hearkeneth unto me (wisdom) shall dwell safely, and shall be quiet from fear of evil.

Using words of discretion, prudence, subtlety and common sense, she turned the situation around to her advantage.

Today's Christian, needs to be more like Abigail. We must open our eyes and be sober to the potential traps Satan constantly devises for our destruction.

I have found that far too often, Christians can be so *heavenly minded* that they are of no earthly good. This not only sets a bad example to those who watch us in the world, but it leaves the Church wide open to the attacks by Satan.

God has placed in each of us a mind to rationalize our everyday situations. He has made available to us the gift of *Sophia*-wisdom to "see" down the road, and the *Phronesis* power to avoid every hurdle. Yet to put these gifts to work in our lives is not only to our advantage, it is our right *and responsibility as Christians!*

If you diligently strive to practice these gifts, you will ultimately find that,

> discretion will watch over you; understanding will guard you; delivering you from the way of evil.
> Proverbs 2:11-12 RSV

Upon awaking from a long night of wine and frivolity, Nabal was told the story of David's narrowly aborted raid. Hearing this shocking news, the rich man was suddenly gripped with fear, and suddenly the stabbing pain of a heart attack overtook him. Ten days later, after Nabal had suffered much, his life of folly ended.

> When David heard that Nabal was dead, he said, "Blessed be the Lord who has avenged the insult I received at the hand of Nabal, and has kept back his servant from evil; the Lord has returned the evil-doing of Nabal upon his own head." Then David sent and wooed Abigail to make her his wife . . .
>
> 1 Samuel 25:39 RSV

The assistance of wisdom's second attribute can defuse your problems today just as easily as it helped to solve Abigail's many years ago. All it takes is for you to open your eyes and see that you cannot handle the tribulations of this world by yourself.

On the obstacle course of this life, you need to wear the practical, common-sense shoes of God's *Phronesis*.

SUNESIS:
Knowledge of the Senses

"...Smelling the incense, listening to the chants and seeing the idol, the apostle instantly realized what to do."

CHAPTER
VII

The third of wisdom's three attributes is *Sunesis,* which the Greek defines as understanding, insight, a running together, (or as we would say today, putting two and two together). This enlightening department of knowledge focuses its power on the body of man. It is the wisdom of tangible things. It deals with the knowledge acquired from our five natural senses.

From the moment you are born, to the day you draw your last breath, you are learning. Everything you touch, smell, taste, see and hear is filed away into that vast storehouse called the brain. This accumulation of *Sunesis-*knowledge influences every thought, action and decision you make. It compares your past experiences and "filed away" knowledge with your present situation. And the sum of this "two plus two" formula affects the decision you will ultimately make.

Consider the unique problem the apostle Paul faced as he walked through the Athenian court atop Mars' Hill.

There, in that hall of higher learning, the apostle watched in disgust as this so-called "civilized" society bowed itself in worship to a family of carved, marble gods. As Acts 17:16 describes it,

> ...his spirit was stirred in him, when he saw the city wholly given to idolatry.

Witnessing this sight Paul no doubt felt the overwhelming urge to lash out at the top of his voice and rebuke these "learned" citizens for their ignorant practices. But his sense of *discretion* held his emotions in check, until he could *wisely* devise a proper plan of action.

Paul knew, by the ultimate knowledge of *Sophia*, that his life's mission was to proclaim the Gospel of Jesus Christ. He had learned, by *Phronesis*, that the most practical way of delivering that message was *to reach people on their own level* and in their own language. Recalling these "filed away" facts, the apostle's *Sunesis* mind quickly went to work.

As a haze of pagan incense and chanting filled Paul's natural senses, wisdom's third facet devised a way for him to fulfill his ultimate purpose. It was a simple plan, bold yet practical. It was subtle, effective and nothing short of ingenious:

> Then Paul stood in the midst of Mars' Hill, and said, Ye men of Athens, I perceive that in all things ye are too superstitious.
>
> For as I passed by, and beheld your devotions, I found an altar with this inscription, TO THE UNKNOWN GOD. Whom therefore ye ignorantly worship, him declare I unto you.

God that made the world and all things therein, seeing that he is Lord of heaven and earth, dwelleth not in temples made with hands;

Neither is worshipped with men's hands, as though he needed any thing, seeing he giveth to all life, and breath, and all things;...

...For in him we live, and move, and have our being; as certain also of your own poets have said, For we are also his offspring.

Forasmuch then as we are the offspring of God, we ought not to think that the Godhead is like unto gold, or silver, or stone, graven by art and man's device.

And the times of this ignorance God winked at; but now commandeth all men everywhere to repent:

Because he hath appointed a day in which he will judge the world in righteousness by that man who he hath ordained; whereof he hath given assurance unto all men, in that he hath raised him from the dead.

And when they heard of the resurrection of the dead, some mocked: and others said, We will hear thee again of this matter.

Acts 17:22-25,28-32

Standing alone in that Greek court, Paul faced a potentially hostile audience. The Athenians were a people raised from birth to believe in the power of their graven gods. To be told blatantly that they were wrong would not only have turned them off to anything Paul had to say, it most certainly would have endangered the apostle's life, as well.

Still, Paul was not about to walk away after witnessing such idolatry. Instead he summoned, from within himself, the assistance of God's understanding, and there, in that great hall, wisdom's three forms went into action.

The *Sophia*-knowledge in Paul's spirit urged him to hold his ground and speak. The practical *Phronesis*-understanding in his conscious mind *pointed out the potential dangers* and *showed him how* to defuse the atmosphere with common sense. But in this particular situation, it was the influence of *Sunesis* that made the difference.

By applying this feature of wisdom to his five natural senses, Paul was able to *wisely evaluate* his surroundings. *Smelling* the incense, *listening* to the monotone chants and *seeing* the idol-filled hall, the apostle instantly realized what to do. With the shrewdness of wisdom, he decided to use one of the Greek's own pagan idols *to prove* both the existence, the power and ultimate superiority of the One and only true God.

By using the Athenian's altar to the unknown God as his "visual aid," Paul was able to capture and hold their collective attention. He was able to communicate with them.

Through the use of this shrewd ploy of wisdom, the apostle Paul's eloquent, well-chosen words were able to sway the deep-rooted opinions of the crowd to his advantage. And in doing so, he managed to fulfill, for that hour, the divine plan for his life, proclaiming the name of Jesus Christ.

This third attribute of wisdom, *Sunesis,* is a teacher. It instructs through the five natural senses in much the same manner as a parent teaches a child through correction.

If Billy is told to "take out the trash" and he fails to do so, his father is then forced to teach him a lesson through punishment. Whether it takes the form of revoked privileges or a spanking, the boy soon learns that if the garbage is *not* removed, either his rights or the sense of feeling in his backside will be! One way or another, obedience is a lesson he will most certainly "file away."

No doubt, when he is faced once again by his father and this dirty chore, Billy will compare his stored-up knowledge of that past experience, with his father's intimidating glare. And quickly evaluating the situation, his *"Sunesis* mind" will happily decide to pick up the garbage cans and take them out to the street.

The wisdom of *Sunesis* is indeed a valuable attribute. It teaches us how to deal with today's tribulations using the combined knowledge of our senses and experiences. Its evaluating instincts can literally make a world of difference in the outcome of your present situation.

However, power of *Sunesis* is only potent when it is linked with *Sophia's* spiritual insights and the practical applications of *Phronesis. These three attributes are a combined force.*

Look at it this way: if you have the *shell* of an egg, you do *not* have an egg. If the whites of an egg are all you have, you *still* don't have an egg. Even if you possess both the *whites* and the *shell*, the "yolk's" on you because you have *yet* to own a *complete* egg. However, if you have the *whites*, the *yolk* and the *shell intact*, then and only then do you truly have an egg.

This same truth applies to God's gift of understanding. To possess the full complement of the Creator's divine knowledge, you must seek after and acquire *all three* of wisdom's facets. When you have accomplished this and exhibit the characteristics of *all* of the attributes, *Sophia, Phronesis* and *Sunesis*, then and *only* then will you truly possess the power of wisdom.

But a word of warning: To depend on one of these facets *alone* is both dangerous and unwise. The peril of such a course is that some possess only the *Sophia*-knowledge of their ultimate goal, and none of the *Phronesis*-understanding of how to reach it. Others have plenty of practical preparation, but no idea of their ultimate purpose. There *must* be a balance!

Those who strive to be wise seek out the Lord's ultimate goal for their life (*Sophia*). They work out the practical path to reach that goal (using God's *Phronesis* guidance), and then plot their daily course with the wise evaluations of *Sunesis*.

Without the combined, balanced power of God's divine understanding, we *cannot* effectively battle the forces of evil. Without the full complement of God's wisdom, we are nothing more than empty eggshells just waiting to be crushed under the feet of Satan. But praise be to Almighty

God! There is a way out. Man has been given an example to follow.

Back at the beginning of all things, the very wisdom we have been discussing enabled the Creator to devise a master plan for man's redemption. In that plan, the Lord provided a means by which man was afforded a divine example to follow, an ultimate role model for living.

> For God so loved the world, that he gave his only begotten Son...
>
> John 3:16

Not only is He our Savior, our Healer and our Counselor, He is also our Standard, our Benchmark, our Supreme Example and our Guide. If God the Father is the Source of all wisdom, then there is no one more capable and worthy to display the full range of wisdom's gift than He who is *One* with the Father, God's only Son, Jesus our Lord.

Christ acknowledged this fact himself, when he said, ...**for she (the Queen of Sheba) came from the uttermost parts of the earth to hear the wisdom of Solomon; and, behold, a greater than Solomon is here. (Matt. 12:42).**

Throughout his 33 years on earth, Jesus not only outclassed Solomon's application and capacity for wisdom, He displayed to the world a higher level and wider expanse of the gift than ever before witnessed. He used the tool of wisdom to its *fullest* potential.

To accomplish this, Christ added to the three combined attributes of understanding an "enhancer," a unique element of wisdom which is, in effect, a powerful spiritual weapon. *Undetectable, especially when used properly, this "secret" weapon has been used by both sides of the spiritual world to inflict galaxy-shaking blows.*

Its first recorded use was by a certain sly serpent in Eden's garden. But Jesus, full of wisdom, found a *positive use* for it Himself. In Christ's hands, this tool transformed wisdom into an indestructible weapon that both confused and confounded the enemy. This powerful force knocked Satan's plans off balance and *turned the tables* on his evil schemes.

In Christ's hands, this *enhanced* wisdom brought salvation's plan to a dying world and helped to win the final battle for man at Calvary's tomb.

By using this "secret" weapon, this simple element of wisdom called *subtlety,* Jesus Christ beat the devil at his own game! Combined with wisdom's three attributes, and using Christ as the ultimate example, this *subtle* source can do the very same for the church today.

Christ's Wisdom:
The Foundation
of the Church

"...Christ saw the serpent behind their smiles..."

CHAPTER
VIII

The needle of the spiritual Richter scale is already registering the coming shake-up. Therefore it is critical that we turn our eyes from the physical world (that the disciples admired, as we saw in Luke 21), and give our attention to the spiritual realm that Jesus pointed out. We must look to Him for wisdom and guidance in the coming days.

Even though we might be committed to rescuing the world from the clutches of Satan, and possess the endurance of a long-distance runner, if we don't have the advantages of a wise, godly strategy, we don't have a chance. If we don't learn how to evaluate our spiritual surroundings and acquire the wisdom to recognize Satan's crafty ploys, we may one day find ourselves the unwitting victim of a demonic sneak attack.

The tribulations that come from such a blind assault can be both devastating and life changing. Just ask Esau.

As soon as Isaac had finished blessing Jacob and Jacob was scarcely gone out from the presence of Isaac his father, Esau his brother came in from his hunting.

Esau had also prepared savory food, and brought it to his father, and said to him, Let my father arise, and eat of his son's game, that you may bless me.

And Isaac his father said to him, Who are you? And he replied, I am your son, your first-born, Esau.

Then Isaac trembled and shook violently, and he said, Who? Where is he who has hunted game and brought it to me, and I ate of it all before you came, and I have blessed him? Yes, and he shall be blessed.

When Esau heard the words of his father, he cried out with a great and bitter cry, and said to his father, Bless me, even me also, O my father!

[Isaac] said, Your brother came with crafty cunning and treacherous deceit, and has taken your blessing.

[Esau] replied, Is he not rightly named Jacob [the supplanter]? For he has supplanted me these two times: he took away my birthright; and now he has taken away my blessing! Have you not still a blessing reserved for me?

And Isaac answered Esau, Behold, I have made [Jacob] your lord and master; I have given all his brethren to him for servants; and with corn and [new] wine have I sustained him. What then can I do for you my son?

Esau said to his father, Have you only one blessing, my father? Bless me, even me also, O my

father! And Esau [could not control] his voice and
wept aloud.

                              Genesis 27:30-38 AMP

This is a sad story, but no one is to blame but Esau.
Jacob, his younger brother, saw the opportunity to take
the advantage — and he took it. Utilizing the negative side
of wisdom's subtlety, Jacob, and his mother Rebekah,
devised a ruse to trick Isaac into imparting the all-
important blessing of the firstborn on the younger.

Esau should have seen it coming. He had already been
tricked once by his deceitful brother, when he foolishly
traded away his eternal birthright for the temporary solace
of a bowl of soup.

> And Esau said to Jacob, I beg of you, let me have
> some of that red lentil stew to eat, for I am faint and
> famished! That is why his name was called Edom (red).
> Jacob answered, Then sell me today your birthright
> — the rights of a first-born.
>
> Esau said, See here, I am at the point of death;
> what good can this birthright do me?
>
> Jacob said, Swear to me today [that you are selling
> it to me]; and he swore to Jacob and sold him his
> birthright.
>
> Then Jacob gave Esau bread and stew of lentils,
> and he ate and drank, and rose up and went his way.
> Thus Esau scorned his birthright as beneath his notice.
>
>   Genesis 25:30-34 AMP

Esau was more interested in his physical welfare than
in his spiritual birthright. Likewise, if we are not careful,
we can become so entangled with the temporal, physical

survival of this world, that we lose our sense of value for Christ's spiritual sustenance.

We must look to Christ in all of our endeavors. Jesus knows how to handle the crafty tricks of Satan. He is the Master at turning the tables on the deceiver, because our Lord and Savior is Wisdom personified.

Throughout His earthly ministry, the eyes of the Son of God were always open, and his mind was perpetually keen and alert. He knew that the subtlety of Satan could take on any form — as it did with Eve in the garden.

Then went the Pharisees, and took counsel how they might entangle him in his talk.

And they sent out unto him their disciples with the Herodians, saying, Master, we know that thou are true, and teachest the way of God in truth, neither carest thou for any man: for thou regardest not the person of men.

Tell us, therefore, What thinkest thou? Is it lawful to give tribute unto Caesar, or not?

But Jesus perceived their wickedness, and said, Why tempt me, ye hypocrites?

Shew me the tribute money. And they brought unto him a penny.

And he saith unto them, Whose is this image and superscription?

They say unto him, Caesar's. Then saith he unto them, Render, therefore unto Caesar the things which are Caesar's; and unto God the things that are God's.

> When they heard these words, they marveled,
> and left him, and went their way.
>
> Matthew 22:15-22

The subtle form Satan took on this occasion was that of the scheming Pharisees and their disciples. Though their words were flattering and their question seemingly valid, the wisdom of Jesus instantly saw through their disguise.

By the spiritual attribute of *Sophia,* Christ saw the serpent behind their smiles. His *Phronesis* mind quickly discerned their evil intent and perceived the potential "trap" of ignoring them.

Upon evaluating the situation (*Sunesis*), Christ *subtlety* requested a look at the currency in question. By this act, he was able to "slyly" turn the tables on his enemy and ensnare the Pharisee's errand boys with the *very object* of their intended trap.

Christ maneuvered Himself into a position of advantage in much the same way that a chess player slyly moves his pieces around the board to confound his opponent and ultimately win the game.

That goal, "winning the game," must be the intent and desire of every Christian. As the Church of Jesus Christ, we must strive to learn God's winning strategy. Because we are confronted daily by the tribulations of Satan, it is *imperative* that we possess the divine know-how to fight fire with fire!

But sadly, it seems that many in the Church today do not have a *subtle* bone in their body. If some poor soul should dare to come to them for counseling or prayer, the first thing they do — before even knowing the situation

— is hit them over the head with the Bible! Too few possess the wise discretion and prudence to evaluate individual circumstances *first,* to avoid capsizing a wounded soul.

If, for instance, someone is suffering from hunger, how is he expected to "hear" the Gospel over the rumbling of his tummy? The *wise* thing to do is feed the physical hunger *first,* so that the heart will be free of distraction. *Then* will the man be ready to hear, understand and accept the bread of eternal life.

Another area where the Christian community lacks subtlety is in its approach to evangelism. As with Paul on Mars' Hill, not everyone is ready immediately to accept *your* theology. Prudence, wisdom, and subtlety must be as much a part of your arsenal of ministry as the Bible itself!

The devil can spot an "unwise" Christian a mile away! In the time it takes for that brother or sister to approach one of his followers, Satan can put up a wall of opposition that the indiscreet can never break through.

There is nothing wrong with blatantly proclaiming your faith; that is the prime directive of God to His Church. Nevertheless, we must learn *how* to wisely communicate that Gospel so as to reach *everyone* effectively.

As the apostle Paul put it,

> For though I be free from all men, yet have I made myself servant unto all, that I might gain the more.
>
> And unto the Jews, I became a Jew that I might gain the Jews; . . . .

> To the weak became I as weak, that I might gain
> the weak: I am made all things to all men, that I might
> by all means save some.

> 1 Corinthians 9:19,20,22

When you acquire the subtlety of *Sunesis*, which Paul used so eloquently, you will instinctively evaluate your daily situations and take into account the personalities and backgrounds of those around you. Utilizing the "two plus two" formula of *Sunesis*, you will automatically consider all of the variables of a given circumstance and instantly devise the *wisest* approach to introducing salvation's plan to others. Time after time, throughout the New Testament, the Son of God beat the devil at his own game by using this tool of subtlety to wisely proclaim the good news of salvation.

One of the best examples of Christ putting this "enhancer" of wisdom into action is on the occasion of his conversation with the Samaritan woman at Jacob's well. Seeing her approach the well to draw water, Jesus asked the woman for a drink. In this situation, His question was more than just a request (noting that the Jews and the Samaritans of this time traditionally kept their distance from each other). Christ's small petition was a wise icebreaker.

> Then saith the woman of Samaria unto him, How
> is it that thou, being a Jew, asketh drink of me, which
> am a woman of Samaria? for the Jews have no dealings
> with the Samaritans.

> Jesus answered and said unto her, If thou knewest
> the gift of God, and who it is that is saith to thee, Give

me a drink; thou wouldest have asked of him, and he would have given thee living water.

The woman saith unto him, Sir, thou hast nothing to draw with, and the well is deep: from whence then hast thou that living water?

Art thou greater than our father Jacob, which gave us the well, and drank thereof himself, and his children, and his cattle?

Jesus answered and said unto her, Whosoever drinketh of this water shall thirst again:

But whosoever drinketh of the water that I shall give him shall never thirst; but the water that I shall give him shall be in him a well of water springing up into everlasting life.

The woman saith unto him, Sir, give me this water, that I thirst not, neither come hither to draw.

Jesus saith unto her, Go, call thy husband, and come hither.

The woman answered and said, I have no husband. Jesus said unto her, Thou hast well said, I have no husband:

For thou hast had five husbands; and he whom thou now hast is not thy husband: in that saidst thou truly.

The woman saith unto him, Sir, I perceive that thou art a prophet...I know that Messias cometh, which is called Christ: when he is come, he will tell us all things.

Jesus saith unto her, I that speak unto thee am he.

> The woman then left her waterpot, and went her way into the city, and saith to the men,
>
> Come, see a man, which told me all things that ever I did. . . And many of the Samaritans of that city believed on him for the saying of the woman which testified, He told me all that I ever did.
>
> John 4:9-19,25,26,28,29,39

Instantly evaluating the Samaritan's situation, Jesus could easily have scorned and condemned her adulterous lifestyle. However, that would have put her on the defensive and hindered her from *honestly* listening to His words. Instead, after getting her attention with His wise, ice-breaking question, Jesus captured her interest and brought her around to the subject He wanted to discuss, by using the illustration of the very water she had come to draw.

By divine knowledge, the Son of God knew the gross iniquity of her past, yet He also realized that the satisfaction she *really craved* could be given to her only *if* she openly admitted her sin and willingly voiced her desire for Christ's living water.

And how did He maneuver her to that place? After hearing her voice her sincere need for that living water, Christ told her, ". . . Go call your husband, and come here."

Now, Jesus knew full well that the Samaritan had no husband, but he used this wise, subtle approach to open the door for her to admit it herself! And when she willingly did so, Jesus Christ, as well, readily revealed Himself to her.

The Church of today needs wisdom, which can be a mighty tool to knock down Satan's walls of opposition.

Wisdom can turn the tables on his crafty schemes and turn tribulation into triumph. Yet, most importantly, wisdom can open the door for others, that Jesus might be revealed.

However, to attain this gift of God, you must, like the Samaritan woman, admit your need, voice your desire and then simply — ask.

Are We Ready?

"The example the Church sets . . . drives men to either get right with God, or to get *left* behind."

CHAPTER
IX

In the middle of an old-fashioned country church testimony service, an old man placed his quivering hand on the pew in front of him, and pulled his tired body to its feet. Seeing the frail gentleman rise, the pastor of the small congregation smiled, gestured in his direction and asked, "And what has the Lord done for you, sir?"

A broad grin came across the man's furrowed face, and his bespectacled eyes lit up with the memories of a lengthy lifetime. "I just want to thank God," his weak voice strained, "in 78 years I've never been down."

A young fellow, sitting nearby, wrinkled his brow upon hearing those words. The old man's testimony was disappointing. It wasn't what he expected to hear.

After the service, as the small group began to file out of the modest sanctuary, the young fellow caught up with the slow-moving gentleman and asked, "How you can claim what you said back there? I don't understand. I've been doing everything I can to follow the Lord, yet I've been down seven times — this week!"

Looking up at the young man's puzzled frown, the venerable Christian grinned just a little, "Son, it's all a matter of perspective," he began, patting his wrinkled hand against the boy's smooth face, "I'm always up, or gettin' up."

The Christian church of today can learn a lot from this wise old saint. Although he was frail, and had seen many a hard time, he had the attitude and spiritual endurance of a long distance runner. He had stopped paying attention to his status in the temporal, physical world and turned his thoughts to the eternal things of the spirit. *That,* my friends, should be the goal of us *all*!

We have to develop a desire to walk daily in the Spirit. Without the heavenly connection, we are ill-equipped to face the hurdles that Satan constantly throws in our path. We need to be so in tune with God, that when the devil *does* try his sneak attacks, we'll be both *ready* — and *able* to surprise him with a few tricks of our own.

The Church of today needs to be more like the prophets and those first courageous Christians. They handled their tribulations with faith. They weathered their storms with determination. And when they were forced to look death in the face, they did not flinch, but they boldly proclaimed the *certainty* of eternal life.

When I think about how those brave souls triumphed over their tribulations and I see how we complain today, I can't help but wonder if the foundation of the Church will be *strong enough* and *smart enough* to withstand the shaking that is soon to come.

Back when Jesus first sent his disciples out into the world, he described them as being "...sheep among wolves." (Matt. 10:16.) The times may change, and the tactics may vary, but the war that was raging then, is still being waged today. And I fear that if we don't wise up to Satan's schemes and stop bleating like lost sheep, the Church is going to end up bleeding like a slaughtered lamb. Let's stop wasting our time outside the temple and start working to bring the lost inside.

Jesus Christ is looking for committed Christians who are *certain* of their convictions, and willing — without hesitation — to stand up for their beliefs. He wants those with the tenacity to stand their ground, no matter whose toes they have to step on. The Lord is searching for a Church whose members will voluntarily stick their neck out when necessary — even if a chopping block awaits in the shadows.

The example the Church sets during adversity drives men either to get *right* with God, or to get *left* behind. The world is *our* responsibility! The way we handle our tribulations helps us to learn not only *of* God and *from* God, but also enables us to teach others *about* God, so that many will be drawn *to* God.

To do all of this effectively involves more than long-suffering. It requires the judicious control of wisdom. Whether we are trying to overcome a problem, discern a ruse of the devil, or win a wounded soul to Christ, the power of godly knowledge should be "standard issue" in today's spiritual struggle. It is the one weapon that is consistently capable of turning the tables on the deceiver. To survive the tremors of tribulations that are coming, we've got to be strong. But to win in the end, we have to be *smart*.

There is a shaking on the way. We must be prepared. Adversity makes the strong stronger — and the weak weaker. I intend to endure. I am determined to not to be under the rubble of impurity that is left behind.

Are you ready? Have you checked your foundation? Have you tapped into the spiritual power that formed the universe out of nothing? Are you ready and willing to go out into the world and rescue the hurting?

We don't have much time. The needle of the Richter scale is moving. Before the next stone falls, let's shore up our crumbling structure and start thinking like Christians again.

Let's take our cue from that old-fashioned church testifier and start shouting out loud, right in the devil's face, "I'm always up..or gettin' up!"

Rod Parsley began his ministry as an energetic 21-year-old, in the backyard of his parent's Ohio home. The fresh, "old-time gospel" approach of Parsley's delivery immediately attracted a hungry, God-seeking audience. From the 17 people who attended that first 1977 backyard meeting, the crowds grew rapidly.

Today, as the pastor of Columbus, Ohio's 5,200 seat World Harvest Church, Parsley oversees World Harvest's K-12 Christian Academy; a growing Bible Institute; and numerous church sponsored outreaches including "*Lifeline*," a pro-life organization, "*Lightline*," an anti-pornography league, and "*Breakthrough*," World Harvest Church's daily and weekly television broadcast, currently on 160 stations and three satellite networks across America.

Pastor Rod Parsley also serves as Dr. Lester Sumrall's personal assistant in directing the End-Time "Feed The Hungry" program.

To contact Rod Parsley,
write:

World Harvest Church
P. O. Box 32932
Columbus, Ohio 43232

*Please include your prayer requests
and comments when you write.*